21st Century
Basic Skills
Library

EARTHQUAKES!

by Cecilia Minden, PhD

Cherry Lake Publishing • Ann Arbor, Michigan

2

Published in the United States of America
by Cherry Lake Publishing
Ann Arbor, Michigan
www.cherrylakepublishing.com

Photo Credits: Cover and page 1, ©iStockphoto.com/hepatus;
page 4, ©Denise Mondloch; page 6, ©SimpleStock/Alamy; page 8,
©Kip Evans/Alamy; page 10, ©iStockphoto.com/Xieyouding; page 12,
©Qing Ding/Shutterstock; page 14, ©David R. Frazier Photolibrary, Inc./
Alamy; page 16, ©JGW Images/Shutterstock; page 18, ©amana
images inc./Alamy; page 20, ©iStockphoto.com/ArtisticCaptures

Library of Congress Cataloging-in-Publication Data
Minden, Cecilia.
  Earthquakes/by Cecilia Minden.
      p. cm.—(21st century basic skills library level 2)
  Includes bibliographical references and index.
  ISBN-13: 978-1-60279-864-9 (lib. bdg.)
  ISBN-10: 1-60279-864-8 (lib. bdg.)
  1. Earthquakes—Juvenile literature. I. Title. II. Series.
  QE521.3.M56 2010
  551.22—dc22   2009048575

Cherry Lake Publishing would like to acknowledge
the work of The Partnership for 21st Century Skills.
Please visit www.21stcenturyskills.org for more information.

Printed in the United States of America
Corporate Graphics Inc.
July 2010
CLFA07

TABLE OF CONTENTS

It's an Earthquake!

The ground is moving. It's an **earthquake**!

Why do earthquakes happen? What can you do?

The places where the pieces fit together are called **faults**.

Sometimes the pieces move.

Then there is an earthquake.

The **epicenter** is the spot above an earthquake.

This is where the ground moves.

Aftershocks come next.

Aftershocks are smaller earthquakes.

They follow a big earthquake.

People **measure** the **magnitude** of an earthquake.

One stronger than 5.0 can hurt people and buildings.

What Can You Do?

What can you do when an earthquake happens?

Drop, cover, and hold on!

Drop to the floor.

Crawl under something big to keep things from falling on you.

Wait until it stops before you move.

Earthquakes only last a few minutes.

Now you are safe!

Find Out More

BOOK

Bauer, Marion Dane and John Wallace (illustrator). *Earthquake!*
  New York: Aladdin, 2009.

WEB SITE
USGS Earthquakes for Kids
earthquake.usgs.gov/learning/kids/
Discover facts, puzzles, and games about earthquakes.

Glossary

aftershocks (AF-tur-shokss) small earthquakes that come soon after a stronger earthquake in the same place

earthquake (URTH-kwayk) a sudden shaking of the ground caused by movement of Earth's top layer

epicenter (EP-uh-sent-ur) the area directly above the place where an earthquake occurs

faults (FAWLTSS) large cracks in Earth's surface that can be the sources of earthquakes

layers (LAY-urz) thicknesses of something lying on top of or under one another

magnitude (MAG-nuh-tood) the size of an earthquake

measure (MEZH-ur) to find out the size of something

Home and School Connection

Use this list of words from the book to help your child become a better reader. Word games and writing activities can help beginning readers reinforce literacy skills.

a	falling	minutes	then
above	faults	move	there
aftershocks	few	moves	they
an	fit	moving	things
and	floor	next	this
are	follow	now	to
before	from	of	together
big	ground	on	top
called	happen	only	under
can	happens	pieces	until
come	hold	places	up
cover	in	safe	wait
crawl	is	smaller	what
do	it	something	when
drop	it's	sometimes	where
Earth	keep	spot	why
earthquake	last	stops	you
earthquakes	layers	that	
epicenter	made	the	

Index

About the Author

Cecilia Minden is the former Director of the Language and Literacy Program at the Harvard Graduate School of Education. She currently works as a literacy consultant for school and library publishers and is the author of more than 100 books for children.